Christmas Around the World

SWEDEN

Find our books at Amazon, Barnes & Noble, Walmart, Target, IngramSpark, Lulu and more!

www.SlothDreamsBooks.com

www.ThePictureBookPro.org
www.SlothDreamsBooks.com

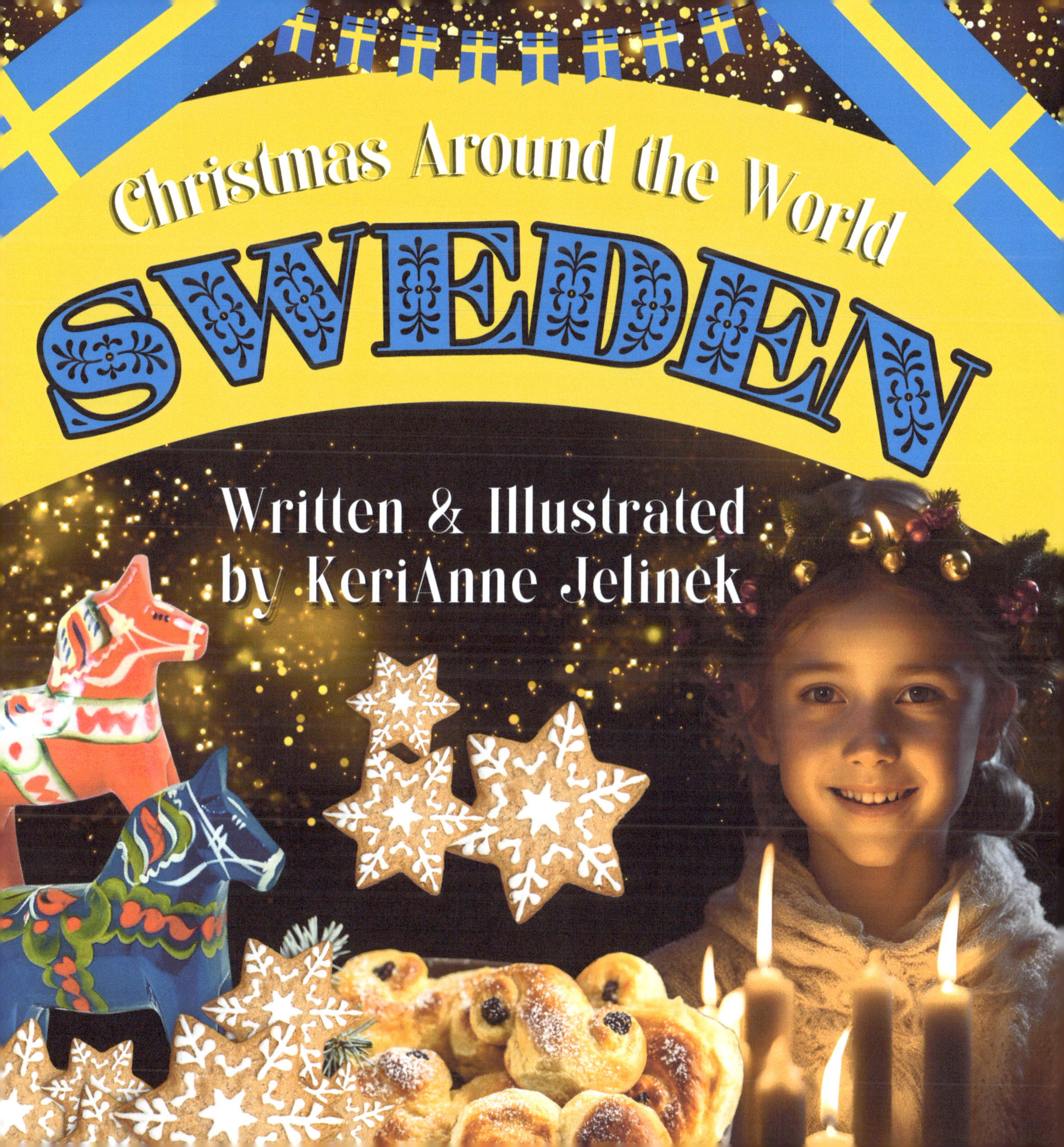

Christmas Around the World
SWEDEN
Written & Illustrated
by KeriAnne Jelinek

Sankta Lucia Day

Sankta Lucia Day is celebrated on December 13th. It's a special day in Sweden that marks the start of the Christmas season.

On this day, people remember Saint Lucia, a brave girl who brought light to others during dark times.

Modern Depiction
of Saint Lucia
Medieval Depiction
of Saint Lucia

Saint Lucia's Story

Saint Lucia was a young girl who lived a long time ago. She was known for her kindness and courage. Saint Lucia helped persecuted Christians hiding in dark catacombs by bringing them food.

She wore a wreath of candles on her head to light her way, so her hands were free to carry food.

Lucia's Procession

During Sankta Lucia celebrations, girls dress up as Lucia wearing white gowns with red sashes and candle wreaths on their heads.

Boys dress up as "star boys" with white robes and star hats. They walk in a procession, singing beautiful songs and spreading joy.

Lussekatter Buns

Lussekatter are delicious saffron buns baked for Sankta Lucia Day. These buns are shaped like curled-up cats with raisin eyes.

The yellow color comes from saffron, which represents the light of Lucia.

Lussekatter Buns

Roots of Sankta Lucia

The tradition of Sankta Lucia has roots in both Christian and ancient Scandinavian customs that originated with the early vikings.

It's a way to bring light during the dark winter days and remember the brave deeds of Saint Lucia.

Vikings
Christian Church
Saint Lucia
Viking Boat Burning Custom

Christmas Season

Christmas, or "Jul" in Sweden, is celebrated from December 24th to January 13th.

It's a time filled with joy, family gatherings, and festive traditions.

God Jul

Christmas Eve

The biggest celebration in Sweden happens on Christmas Eve, December 24th.

Families come together to decorate the Christmas tree, exchange gifts, and enjoy a special feast.

Christmas Tree (Julgran)

The Christmas tree, or "Julgran," is decorated with ornaments, candles, and straw figures.

One popular ornament is the straw goat called "Julbock," which has ancient Yule traditions.

WASSAIL
GOD
JUL!

Julbord Feast

On Christmas Eve, families enjoy a big feast called "Julbord."

It includes a variety of dishes like herring, meatballs, sausages, and a special Christmas ham called "Julskinka."

Christmas Treats

Swedish Christmas treats include gingerbread cookies known as "Pepparkakor" and rice pudding called "Risgrynsgröt."

It's fun to hide an almond in the rice pudding, and whoever finds it will have good luck!

Jultomten
(Santa Claus)

Jultomten, the Swedish Santa Claus, visits homes on Christmas Eve to give presents.

He often knocks on the door, and children eagerly open it to find him with a sack full of gifts.

DEC 25

Christmas Day

Christmas Day, December 25th, is a time for quiet family moments and reflection.

Many families attend church and spend the day appreciating the beauty of the season.

St. Stephen's Day

December 26th is St. Stephen's Day, or "Annandag Jul," a public holiday in Sweden.

It's a day for visiting friends and family or just relaxing after the Christmas festivities.

26
DECEMBER

God jul

New Year's Eve & Ephiphany

The New Year's Eve celebration, "Nyårsafton," includes fireworks and parties to welcome the new year.

The Epiphany, or "Trettondedag Jul," on January 6th, is another important holiday in Sweden, marking the end of the Christmas season & the Biblical story of the Magi .

06
JANUARY
Epiphany
JANUARY
13

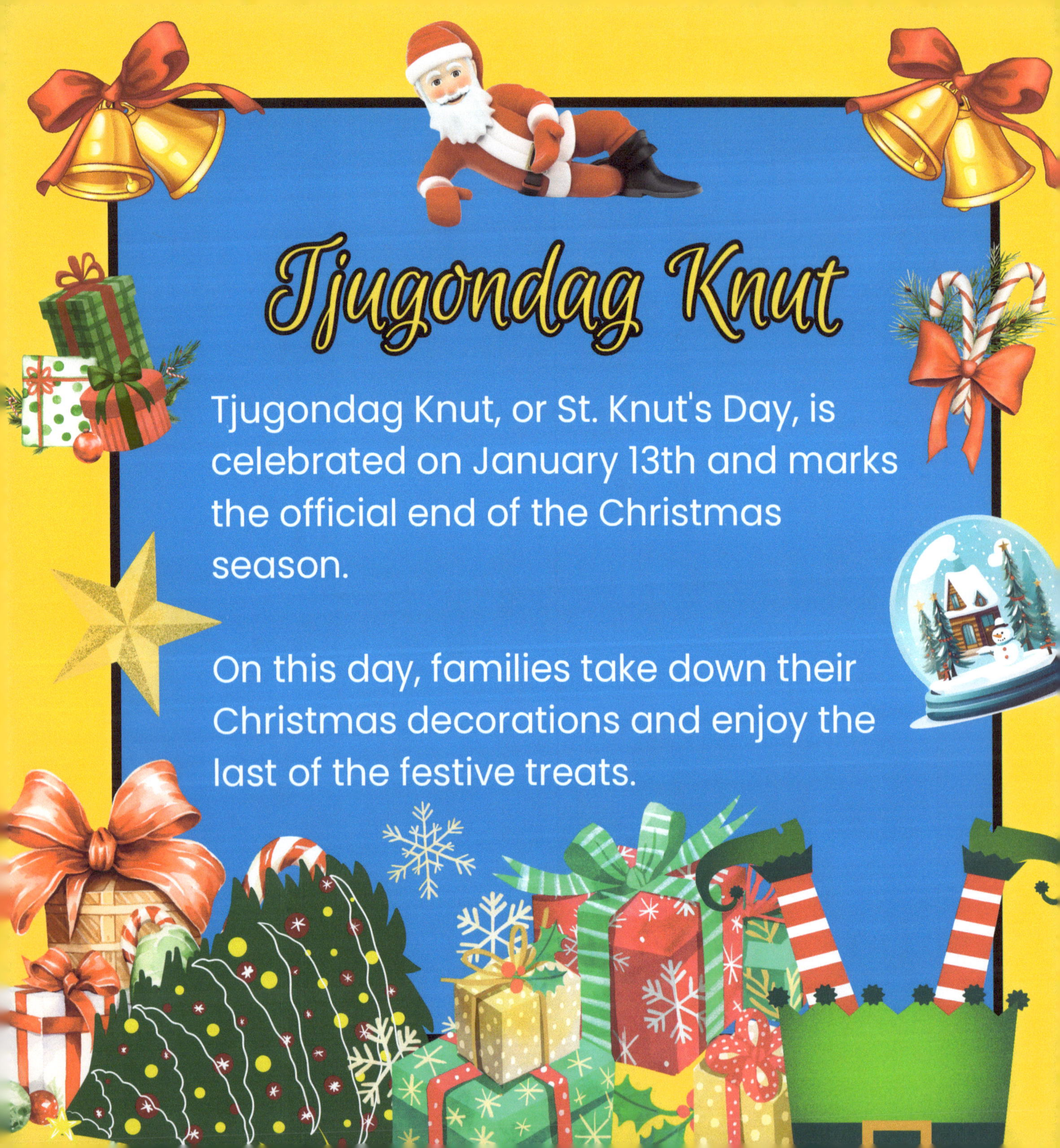

Tjugondag Knut

Tjugondag Knut, or St. Knut's Day, is celebrated on January 13th and marks the official end of the Christmas season.

On this day, families take down their Christmas decorations and enjoy the last of the festive treats.

www.ingramcontent.com/pod-product-compliance
Lightning Source LLC
LaVergne TN
LVHW071653180726
843512LV00002B/448